CUMBRIA HERITAGE SERVICES
LIBRARIES

Cumbria
COUNTY COUNCIL

This book is due to be returned on or before the last date above. It may be renewed by personal application, post or telephone, if not in demand.

C.L.18

Robert Atwell is an Anglican priest. After six years as Chaplain of Trinity College, Cambridge, he became a Benedictine monk, spending the next ten years in a monastery in the Cotswolds.

He is the compiler of two volumes of daily readings for the liturgical year, *Celebrating the Saints* and *Celebrating the Seasons,* both published by the Canterbury Press.

He is presently vicar of the parish of St Mary the Virgin, Primrose Hill, in London.

REMEMBER

100 readings
for those in grief and
bereavement

compiled by
Robert Atwell

CANTERBURY
PRESS
Norwich

© in this compilation Robert Atwell 2005

First published in 2005 by the Canterbury Press Norwich
(a publishing imprint of Hymns Ancient & Modern Limited,
a registered charity)
9–17 St Albans Place, London N1 0NX

www.scm-canterburypress.co.uk

British Library Cataloguing in Publication data

A catalogue record for this book is available
from the British Library

ISBN 1-85311-641-6

Typeset by Regent Typesetting, London
Printed and bound by
Creative Print and Design

Contents

Introduction

One of the things that distinguishes human beings from the rest of the animal kingdom – at least as far as we know – is our capacity to remember. In our minds we find stockpiled all kinds of memories. Our memory contributes to our sense of identity. It is why Alzheimer's Disease is so terrifying, because with the disintegration and loss of our memory we lose a sense of self: we no longer know who we are or who other people are. We find ourselves cast adrift on an internal sea of confusion, distracted by the flotsam and jetsam of fragmented and partial memories. As the wife of a former colleague of mine movingly said of her husband in the latter stages of the disease, 'The lights are on, but there's no one at home.' We are what we remember.

Not only, however, do we have a sense of the past, we also have a sense of the future. Uniquely we live in the knowledge that one day we will die. That inescapable fact shapes our lives, and it casts a deepening shadow on our endeavours as we age. How we come to terms with our mortality is perhaps the single greatest challenge that confronts us as individuals. The death of friends or parents happens to us all sooner or later. Negotiating grief and bereavement is never easy, but in a society that has largely abandoned traditional mourning rituals it has become particularly difficult. The black crepe armbands of our Victorian forebears may have been ostentatious, but at least they put out a signal to neighbours and casual acquaintances that their emotions and reactions were not in equilibrium. By contrast today, people are often expected to bounce back as if nothing has happened and carry on as normal. We learn to hide and suppress our grief, sometimes unhealthily so, and become vulnerable to depression. In such circumstances the loss of something comparatively trivial, or attending another funeral of someone we barely know, brings it all back, triggering in us uncontrollable weeping as at last we give ourselves permission to shed the tears we have bottled up inside for so long. Loss and grief do not obey rules.

This anthology is an assembly of readings and poetry to help people negotiate the lonely journey of bereavement. It is designed to be plundered for readings at a funeral or memorial service or for Remembrance Sunday commemorations. But equally, it is a book that can be left on the bedside table, to be thumbed through in the early hours of the morning when sleep deserts us and old painful memories haunt us. Some of the readings will be familiar, and by their very familiarity be found comforting. Other readings will be new and perhaps challenging. They have sometimes been arranged to complement or contrast with one another. By and large, however, they are not in any particular order, reflecting the disjointed nature of bereavement which touches upon the whole gamut of human emotion: loss, bitterness, love, despair, grief, faith, anger, emptiness, hope. They offer us words and images with which to understand our feelings, and to plot our course. Ultimately, they give us permission to remember, and find solace in so doing.

Robert Atwell

For everything there is a season . . .
a time to be born, and a time to die

Death be not proud

Death be not proud, though some have called thee
  Mighty and dreadful, for, thou art not so,
    For, those, whom thou think'st, thou dost
      overthrow,
Die not, poor Death, nor yet canst thou kill me;
From rest and sleep, which but thy pictures be,
    Much pleasure, then from thee, much more
      must flow;
    And soonest our best men with thee do go,
Rest of their bones, and soul's delivery.
Thou art slave to fate, chance, kings, and desperate men,
    And dost with poison, war, and sickness dwell,
    And poppy, or charms can make us sleep as well,
And better than thy stroke. Why swell'st thou then?
    One short sleep past, we wake eternally,
    And death shall be no more: Death thou shalt die.

John Donne (1571–1631), Holy Sonnet

What is life?

And what is life? An hour-glass on the run
  A mist retreating from the morning sun
  A busy bustling still repeated dream.
Its length? A moment's pause, a moment's thought.
  And happiness? A bubble on the stream
That in the act of seizing shrinks to nought.

Vain hopes – what are they? Puffing gales of morn
That of its charms divests the dewy lawn
  And robs each flower of its gem and dies,
A cobweb hiding disappointments, thorn
  Which stings more keenly thro' the thin disguise.

And thou, O trouble? Nothing can suppose,
And sure the Power of Wisdom only knows,
  What need requireth thee.
So free and lib'ral as thy bounty flows,
  Some necessary cause must surely be.

And what is death? Is still the cause unfound
The dark mysterious name of horrid sound
  A long and ling'ring sleep the weary crave –
And peace – where can its happiness abound?
  Nowhere at all, but heaven and the grave.

Then what is life? When stripped of its disguise
  A thing to be desired it cannot be,
Since everything that meets our foolish eyes
  Gives proof sufficient of its vanity.

'Tis but a trial all must undergo
    To teach unthankful mortals how to prize
That happiness vain man's denied to know,
    Until he's called to claim it in the skies.

John Clare (1793–1864)

Time flies

Time flies, hope flags, life plies a wearied wing;
    Death following hard on life gains ground apace;
  Faith runs with each and rears an eager face,
Outruns the rest, makes light of everything,
Spurns earth, and still finds breath to pray and sing;
    While love ahead of all uplifts his praise,
    Still asks for grace and still gives thanks for grace,
Content with all day brings and night will bring.
Life wanes; and when love folds his wings above
    Tired hope, and less we feel his conscious pulse,
    Let us go fall asleep, dear friend, in peace:
    A little while, and age and sorrow cease;
A little while, and life reborn annuls
Loss and decay and death, and all is love.

Christina Rossetti (1830–94)

By the river

I was tired
  When we found the place,
The quiet place by the river,
Where the sun shines through the willows,
Dappling the dark water
With green and gold.

I thought:
This is the end, this is peace.
We will stay by the river;
We will listen to its soft music
And watch its deep flowing.
The whispering leaves will be silent,
The golden shadows will deepen,
The river will rise and caress us.
Gently it will rise and embrace us
And bear us away, together.

Joyfully
I turned to tell you these things.
But I was alone by the river.
A cold wind shivered the willows;
Slowly a leaf twisted down to the water
And was carried away.

Anna McMullen (1904–)

When to the sessions of sweet silent thought

When to the sessions of sweet silent thought
    I summon up remembrance of things past,
I sigh the lack of many a thing I sought,
    And with old woes new wail my dear time's waste.
Then can I drown an eye, unus'd to flow,
    For precious friends hid in death's dateless night,
And weep afresh love's long since cancell'd woe,
    And moan th'expense of many a vanish'd sight.
Then can I grieve at grievances foregone,
    And heavily from woe to woe tell o'er
The sad account of fore-bemoaned moan,
    Which I new pay as if not paid before.
      But if the while I think on thee, dear friend,
      All losses are restor'd, and sorrows end.

William Shakespeare (1564–1616), Sonnet XXX

The apology of Socrates as he is condemned to die

A soldier put on guard, either at the post which he chose himself as the best to defend, or where his commander put him, has to stay there and run the risks. He knows that nothing is worse than disgrace, not even death.

When I was a soldier in the army, your generals put me in posts in Potidaea and Amphipolis and Delium. Like everyone else I stayed where I was put, and ran the risk of death. And in the same way during my life I have believed and understood that God gave me a vocation; my 'orders' were to spend my life in the study of philosophy, and in trying to discover about myself and others. It would be quite as terrible to leave this post through fear of death or any other danger, as to run away from the enemy when I was a soldier. Terrible is the right word for it. If I deserted this vocation, you could justly have me up in court, and accuse me of being an atheist, and a coward, and of thinking that I am wise when I am not. To be afraid of death is just that – to suppose oneself wise when one is not; it means you think you know what you do not. Death may be the greatest blessing to man – no one knows. If men are afraid of it, they pretend to a knowledge that it is the greatest of ills. No ignorance is worse than to think one knows what one does not know.

Perhaps about this I do differ from other men. If I were to say that I am wiser in anything, it would be here. I do not think that I know much about the other world. What I do know is this: to do wrong is a disgrace; to disobey him who is higher than I, whether he be God or man, is a disgrace. Therefore I shall not fear; I shall not shrink from anything where I have no certainty. The only thing I am certain about is that some things are bad. It is them, and them alone, that I fear.

Plato, *The Apology* (16D–17B)

Do not go gentle into that good night

Do not go gentle into that good night,
Old age should burn and rave at close of day;
Rage, rage against the dying of the light.

Though wise men at their end know dark is right,
Because their words had forked no lightning they
Do not go gentle into that good night.

Good men, the last wave by, crying how bright
Their frail deeds might have danced in a green bay,
Rage, rage against the dying of the light.

Wild men who caught and sang the sun in flight,
And learn, too late, they grieved it on its way,
Do not go gentle into that good night.

Grave men, near death, who see with blinding sight
Blind eyes could blaze like meteors and be gay,
Rage, rage against the dying of the light.

And you, my father, there on the sad height,
Curse, bless, me now with your fierce tears, I pray.
Do not go gentle into that good night.
Rage, rage against the dying of the light.

Dylan Thomas (1914–53)

Abide with me

Abide with me; fast falls the eventide;
The darkness deepens; Lord, with me abide!
When other helpers fail, and comforts flee,
Help of the helpless, O abide with me.

Swift to its close ebbs out life's little day;
Earth's joys grow dim, its glories pass away;
Change and decay in all around I see;
O thou who changest not, abide with me.

I need thy presence every passing hour;
What but thy grace can foil the tempter's power?
Who like thyself my guide and stay can be?
Through cloud and sunshine, O abide with me.

I fear no foe with thee at hand to bless;
Ills have no weight, and tears no bitterness.
Where is death's sting? Where, grave, thy victory?
I triumph still, if thou abide with me.

Hold thou thy cross before my closing eyes;
Shine through the gloom, and point me to the skies:
Heaven's morning breaks, and earth's vain shadows flee;
In life, in death, O Lord, abide with me!

H. F. Lyte (1793–1847)

The hour of our death

We live in a rapidly changing world. Nothing is certain. One thing is: we all face death. It is a sombre thought. We find all sorts of ways of forgetting about it. We use expressions which empty it of finality and threat. We talk about 'going to the other side' or 'passing away'. Yet it is the Christian instinct to be brave and to face the meaning of death fairly and squarely. We face it because it is inescapable, one of life's harsh realities. Whenever a member of the family, or a colleague, dies we are reminded very vividly that it is the one thing which will happen to each one of us. Dying can be a very lonesome experience, for nothing can be more isolating than pain.

One day I shall die. Thinking about that is good for me. It helps me to look at the way I am living. It enables me to get a better perspective. I know that I shall not remain forever in this world. I must ask important questions: 'Am I making the best of my life? Am I living in such a way that I try always to follow my conscience? Are my motives right? What do I really want? What am I really seeking?' Those are very simple and fundamental questions, and ones that we have to ask ourselves. That is a sobering thought. While such thoughts have their value, it would be quite wrong to leave it like that. The Christian faces death realistically, but also knows that death is a gateway, a new beginning, a fulfilment of human life.

It is for that deep joy and happiness that we were made. One day it will be ours . . . We are men and women moving through life like pilgrims towards our final destination. It is healthy to look forward to that destination when we shall find total fulfilment. That fulfilment must consist in an experience of love because love is the highest of all human experience. To love totally, to be loved completely. It is in union with that which is most lovable that we become fully ourselves.

Cardinal Basil Hume (1923–99), *To Be a Pilgrim*

To Emilia

Music, when soft voices die,
  Vibrates in the memory –
Odours, when sweet violets sicken,
Live within the sense they quicken.

Rose leaves, when the rose is dead,
Are heaped for the beloved's bed –
And so thy thoughts, when thou art gone,
Love itself shall slumber on . . .

Percy Bysshe Shelley (1792–1822)

No man is an island

All mankind is of one Author, and is one volume. When one man dies, one chapter is not torn out of the book, but translated into a better language; and every chapter must be so translated. God employs several translators: some pieces are translated by age, some by sickness, some by war, some by justice. But God's hand is in every translation; and his hand shall bind up all our scattered leaves again, for that library where every book shall lie open to one another. As therefore the bell that rings to a sermon calls not upon the preacher only, but upon the congregation to come; so this bell which tolls calls us all.

No man is an island, entire of itself; every man is a piece of the continent, a part of the main. If a clod be washed away by the sea, Europe is the less, as well as if a promontory were, as well as if a manor of thy friends or of thine own were. Any man's death diminishes me, because I am involved in mankind. And therefore never send to know for whom the bell tolls; it tolls for thee.

John Donne (1571–1631), *Devotions upon Emergent Occasions*

I wake and feel the fell of dark

I wake and feel the fell of dark, not day.
  What hours, O what black hours we have spent
This night! what sights you, heart, saw; ways you went!
And more must, in yet longer light's delay.

With witness I speak this. But where I say
Hours I mean years, mean life. And my lament
Is cries countless, cries like dead letters sent
To dearest him that lives alas! away.

I am gall, I am heartburn. God's most deep decree
Bitter would have me taste: my taste was me;
Bones built in me, flesh filled, blood brimmed with curse.

Selfyeast of spirit a dull dough sours. I see
The lost are like this, and their scourge to be
As I am mine, their sweating selves; but worse.

Gerard Manley Hopkins (1844–89)

On my first son

Farewell, thou child of my right hand, and joy;
  My sin was too much hope of thee, loved boy:
Seven years thou 'wert lent to me, and I thee pay,
Exacted by thy fate, on the just day.
O could I lose all father now! For why
Will man lament the state he should envy,

To have so soon 'scaped world's and flesh's rage,
And, if no other misery, yet age?
Rest in soft peace, and asked, say, 'Here doth lie
Ben Johnson his best piece of poetry.'
For whose sake henceforth all his vows be such
As what he loves may never like too much.

Ben Jonson (1572–1637)

On the death of his mother

My mother and I were standing leaning out of a window overlooking a garden. We were staying at Ostia on the Tiber, where, far removed from the crowds, after the exhaustion of a long journey, we were recovering our strength in preparation for our return voyage to Africa. As we talked, my mother said, 'My son, as for myself, I now find no pleasure in this life. What I have still to do here and why I am here, I do not know. My hope in this world is already fulfilled. The one reason why I wanted to stay longer in this life was my desire to see you a Catholic Christian before I die. My God has granted this in a way more than I had hoped. For I see you despising this world's success to become his servant. What have I to do here?'

The reply I made to this I do not well recall, for within five days or not much more she fell sick of a fever. While she was ill, on one day she suffered loss of consciousness and gradually became unaware of things around her. We

[15]

ran to be with her, but she quickly recovered consciousness. She looked at me and my brother standing beside her, and said to us in the manner of someone looking for something, 'Where was I?' Then seeing us struck dumb with grief, she said: 'Bury your mother here.'

I kept silence and fought back my tears. But my brother, as if to cheer her up, said something to the effect that he hoped she would be buried not in a foreign land but in her home country. When she heard that, her face became worried and her eyes looked at him in reproach that he should think that. She looked in my direction and said, 'See what he says,' and soon said to both of us 'Bury my body anywhere you like. Let no anxiety about that disturb you. I have only one request to make of you, that you remember me at the altar of the Lord, wherever you may be.' She explained her thought in such words as she could speak, then fell silent as the pain of her sickness became worse. 'Nothing,' she said, 'is distant from God, and there is no ground for fear that he may not acknowledge me at the end of the world and raise me up.' On the ninth day of her illness, when she was aged fifty-six, and I was thirty-three, this religious and devout soul was released from the body.

St Augustine (354–430), *Confessions*

If I lay here dead

Is it indeed so? If I lay here dead,
    Wouldst thou miss any life in losing mine?
And would the sun of thee more coldly shine
Because of grave-damps falling round my head?
I marvelled, my Belovèd, when I read
Thy thought so in the letter. I am thine –
But . . . so much to thee? Can I pour thy wine
While my hands tremble? Then my soul, instead
Of dreams of death, resumes life's lower range.
Then, love me, Love! Look on me – breathe on me!
As brighter ladies do not count it strange,
For love, to give up acres and degree,
I yield the grave for thy sake, and exchange
My near sweet view of Heaven, for earth with thee!

Elizabeth Barrett Browning (1806–61), *Sonnets from the Portuguese XXIII*

I envy not in any moods

I envy not in any moods
    The captive void of noble rage,
    The linnet born within the cage,
That never knew the summer woods:

I envy not the beast that takes
    His license in the field of time,
    Unfetter'd by the sense of crime,
To whom a conscience never wakes;

Nor, what may count itself as blest,
    The heart that never plighted troth
    But stagnates in the weeds of sloth;
Nor any want-begotten rest.

I hold it true, whate'er befall;
    I feel it, when I sorrow most;
    'Tis better to have loved and lost
Than never to have loved at all.

Alfred, Lord Tennyson (1809–92), *In Memoriam XXVII*

What is dying?

A ship sails and I stand watching till she fades on the horizon, and someone at my side says, 'She is gone'. Gone where? Gone from my sight, that is all; she is just as large as when I saw her. The diminished size and total loss of sight is in me, not in her, and just at the moment when someone at my side says, 'She is gone', there are others who are watching her coming, and other voices take up a glad shout, 'Here she comes!' . . . and that is dying.

Charles Brent (1862–1929)

Departure

It was not like your great and gracious ways!
  Do you, that have nought other to lament,
Never, my Love, repent
Of how, that July afternoon,
You went,
With sudden, unintelligible phrase,
And frighten'd eye,
Upon your journey of so many days,
Without a single kiss, or a good-bye?
I knew, indeed, that you were parting soon;
And so we sat, within the low sun's rays,
You whispering to me, for your voice was weak,
Your harrowing praise.
Well, it was well,
To hear you such things speak,
And I could tell
What made your eyes a growing gloom of love,
As a warm South-wind sombres a March grove.
And it was like your great and gracious ways
To turn your talk on daily things, my Dear,
Lifting the luminous, pathetic lash
To let the laughter flash,
Whilst I drew near,
Because you spoke so low that I could scarcely hear.
But all at once to leave me at the last,
More at the wonder than the loss aghast,
With huddled, unintelligible phrase,
And frighten'd eye,
And go your journey of all days

With not one kiss, or a good-bye,
And the only loveless look the look with which you
　　pass'd:
'Twas all unlike your great and gracious ways.

Coventry Patmore (1823–96)

Old men

People expect old men to die,
　　They do not really mourn old men.
Old men are different. People look
At them with eyes that wonder when . . .
People watch with unshocked eyes;
But the old men know when an old man dies.

Ogden Nash (1902–71)

The despair of old age

The fear of death is one of the faces of despair in old age. This fear is less of annihilation than it is of absurdity. Death comes too soon. It will seal the emptiness of my life before I can make sense of it, before I can make some last attempt to give it meaning.

For the sting of death is not the loss of life, but the loss of meaning.

Finbar Lynch

The old familiar faces

I have had playmates, I have had companions
In my days of childhood, in my joyful schooldays;
All, all are gone, the old familiar faces.

I have been laughing, I have been carousing,
Drinking late, sitting late, with my bosom cronies;
All, all are gone, the old familiar faces.

I loved a love once, fairest among women:
Closed are her doors on me, I must not see her –
All, all are gone, the old familiar faces.

I have a friend, a kinder friend has no man:
Like an ingrate, I left my friend abruptly;
Left him, to muse on the old familiar faces.

Ghost-like I paced round the haunts of my childhood,
Earth seem'd a desert I was bound to traverse,
Seeking to find the old familiar faces.

Friend of my bosom, thou more than a brother,
Why were not thou born in my father's dwelling?
So might we talk of the old familiar faces.

How some they have died, and some they have left me,
And some are taken from me; all are departed;
All, all are gone, the old familiar faces.

Charles Lamb (1775–1834)

Remembrance

Cold in the earth – and the deep snow piled
      above thee,
Far, far, removed, cold in the dreary grave!
Have I forgot, my only Love, to love thee,
Severed at last by Time's all-severing wave?

Now, when alone, do my thoughts no longer hover
Over the mountains, on that northern shore,
Resting their wings where hearth and fern-leaves cover
Thy noble heart for ever, ever more?

Cold in the earth – and fifteen wild Decembers,
From those brown hills, have melted into spring:
Faithful, indeed, is the spirit that remembers
After such years of change and suffering!

Sweet Love of youth, forgive, if I forget thee,
While the world's tide is bearing me along;
Other desires and other hopes beset me,
Hopes which obscure, but cannot do thee wrong!

No later light has lightened up my heaven,
No second morn has ever shone for me;
All my life's bliss from thy dear life was given,
All my life's bliss is in the grave with thee.

But, when the days of golden dreams had perished,
And even Despair was powerless to destroy;
Then did I learn how existence could be cherished,
Strengthened and fed without the aid of joy.

Then did I check the tears of useless passion –
Weaned my young soul from yearning after thine;
Sternly denied its burning wish to hasten
Down to that tomb already more than mine.

And, even yet, I dare not let it languish,
Dare not indulge in memory's rapturous pain;
Once drinking deep of that divinest anguish,
How could I seek the empty world again?

Emily Brontë (1818–48)

Teach me to treat my death as an act of communion

It was a joy to me, O God, in the midst of the struggle, to feel that in developing myself I was increasing the hold that you have upon me; it was a joy to me, too, under the inward thrust of life or amid the favourable play of events, to abandon myself to your providence. Now that I have found the joy of utilising all forms of growth to make you, or to let you, grow in me, grant that I may willingly consent to this last phase of communion in the course of which I shall possess you by diminishing in you.

After having perceived you as he who is 'a greater myself', grant, when my hour comes, that I may recognise you under the species of each alien or hostile force

[23]

that seems bent upon destroying or uprooting me. When the signs of age begin to mark my body (and still more when they touch my mind); when the ill that is to diminish me or carry me off strikes from without or is born within me; when the painful moment comes in which I suddenly awaken to the fact I am losing hold of myself and am absolutely passive within the hands of the great unknown forces that have formed me; in all those dark moments, O God, grant that I may understand that it is you (provided only my faith is strong enough) who are painfully parting the fibres of my being in order to penetrate to the very marrow of my substance and bear me away within yourself.

The more deeply and incurably the evil is encrusted in my flesh, the more it will be you that I am harbouring – you as a loving, active principle of purification and detachment. Vouchsafe, therefore, something more precious still than the grace for which all the faithful pray. It is not enough that I shall die while communicating. Teach me to treat my death as an act of communion.

Pierre Teilhard de Chardin (1881–1955), *Le Milieu Divin*

Go forth upon your journey

Go forth upon your journey from this world,
in the name of God the Father almighty who
created you:
in the name of Jesus Christ who suffered death for you;
in the name of the Holy Spirit who strengthens you;
in communion with the blessed saints,
and aided by angels and archangels,
and all the armies of the heavenly host.
May your portion this day be in peace,
and your dwelling in the heavenly Jerusalem.

Commendation of the Dying (Traditional)

To everything there is a season and a time

To everything there is a season,
and a time to every purpose under the heaven:
a time to be born, and a time to die;
a time to plant, and a time to pluck up that which is
planted;
a time to kill, and a time to heal;
a time to break down, and a time to build up;
a time to weep, and a time to laugh;
a time to mourn, and a time to dance;
a time to cast away stones, and a time to gather stones
together;
a time to embrace, and a time to refrain from
embracing;

a time to get, and a time to lose;
a time to keep, and a time to cast away;
a time to rend, and a time to sew;
a time to keep silence, and a time to speak;
a time to love, and a time to hate;
a time for war, and a time for peace.
What profit hath he that worketh in that wherein he
    laboureth?
I have seen the travail, which God hath given to the
    sons of men to be exercised in it.
He hath made everything beautiful in its time:
also he hath set the world in their heart,
so that no man can find out the work that God
maketh from the beginning to the end.
I know that there is no good in them,
but for a man to rejoice, and to do good in his life.
And also that every man should eat and drink,
and enjoy the good of all his labour,
for it is a gift of God.

Ecclesiastes 3, King James' Bible

God be in my head

God be in my head,
and in my understanding;

God be in mine eyes,
and in my looking;

God be in my mouth,
and in my speaking;

God be in my heart,
and in my loving;

God be at mine end,
and at my departing.

Sarum Primer (1514)

Many waters cannot quench love

Set me as a seal upon your heart,
as a seal upon your arm.
For love is strong as death,
jealousy as cruel as the grave.
Many waters cannot quench love,
neither can the floods drown it.
For love is as strong as death.

The Song of Songs 8, the Bible

Ashes to ashes,
dust to dust

Farewell, sweet dust

Now I have lost you, I must scatter
  All of you on the air henceforth;
Not that to me it can ever matter
But it's only fair to the rest of earth.

Now especially, when it is winter
And the sun's not half so bright as he was,
Who wouldn't be glad to find a splinter
That once was you, in the frozen grass?

Snowflakes, too, will be softer feathered,
Clouds, perhaps, will be whiter plumed;
Rain, whose brilliance you caught and gathered,
Purer silver have reassumed.

Farewell, sweet dust; I was never a miser:
Once, for a minute, I made you mine:
Now you are gone, I am none the wiser
But the leaves of the willow are bright as wine.

Elinor Wylie (1885–1928)

Song

When I am dead, my dearest,
      Sing no sad songs for me;
Plant thou no roses at my head,
      Nor shady cypress tree:
Be the green grass above me
      With showers and dewdrops wet;
And if thou wilt, remember,
      And if thou wilt, forget.

I shall not see the shadows,
      I shall not feel the rain;
I shall not hear the nightingale
      Sing on, as if in pain;
And dreaming through the twilight
      That doth not rise nor set,
Haply I may remember,
      And haply may forget.

Christina Rossetti (1830–94)

On the death of Emily Jane Brontë
24 December 1848

My darling, thou wilt never know
   The grinding agony of woe
     That we have borne for thee.
Thus may we consolation tear
E'en from the depth of our despair
     And wasting misery.

The nightly anguish thou art spared
When all the crushing truth is bared
     To the awakening mind,
When the galled heart is pierced with grief,
Till wildly it implores relief,
     But small relief can find.

Nor know'st thou what it is to lie
Looking forth with streaming eye
     On life's lone wilderness.
'Weary, weary, dark and drear,
How shall I the journey bear,
     The burden and distress?'

Then since thou art spared such pain
We will not wish thee here again;
     He that lives must mourn.
God help us through our misery
And give us rest and joy with thee
     When we reach our bourne!

Charlotte Brontë (1816–55)

Dirge without music

I am not resigned to the shutting away of loving
  hearts in the hard ground.
So it is, and so it will be, for so it has been, time out
  of mind:
Into the darkness they go, the wise and the lovely.
  Crowned
With lilies and with laurel they go; but I am
  not resigned.

Lovers and thinkers, into the earth with you.
Be one with the dull, the indiscriminate dust.
A fragment of what you felt, of what you knew,
A formula, a phrase remains – but the best is lost.

The answers quick and keen, the honest look, the
  laughter, the love –
They are gone. They are gone to feed the roses. Elegant
  and curled
Is the blossom. Fragrant is the blossom. I know. But I
  do not approve.
More precious was the light in your eyes than all the
  roses in the world.

Down, down, down into the darkness of the grave
Gently they go, the beautiful, the tender, the kind;
Quietly they go, the intelligent, the witty, the brave.
I know. But I do not approve. And I am not resigned.

Edna St Vincent Millay (1892–1950)

The secret of death

And he said: You would know the secret of death. But how shall you find it unless you seek it in the heart of life? If you would indeed behold the spirit of death, open your heart wide unto the body of life. For life and death are one, even as the river and the sea are one. In the depth of your hopes and desires lies your silent knowledge of the beyond; and like seeds dreaming beneath the snow your heart dreams of spring.

Trust the dreams, for in them is hidden the gate to eternity. Your fear of death is but the trembling of the shepherd when he stands before the king whose hand is laid upon him in honour: Is not the shepherd joyful beneath his trembling that he shall wear the mark of the king? Yet is he not more mindful of his trembling? For what is it to die but to stand naked in the wind and to melt into the sun? And what is it to cease breathing but to free the breath from its restless tides, that it may rise and expand and seek God unencumbered?

Only when you drink from the river of silence shall you indeed sing. And when you have reached the mountain top, then you shall begin to climb. And when the earth shall claim your limbs, then shall you truly dance.

Khalil Gibran (1883–1931), *The Prophet*

Epitaph on a friend

An honest man here lies at rest,
  The friend of man, the friend of truth,
The friend of age, and guide of youth:
Few hearts like his, with virtue warm'd,
Few heads with knowledge so inform'd;
If there's another world, he lives in bliss;
If there is none, he made the best of this.

Robert Burns (1759–96)

The face of all the world is changed

The face of all the world is changed, I think,
  Since first I heard the footsteps of thy soul
Move still, oh, still, beside me, as they stole
Betwixt me and the dreadful outer brink
Of obvious death, where I, who thought to sink,
Was caught up into love, and taught the whole
Of life in a new rhythm. The cup of dole
God gave for baptism, I am fain to drink,
And praise its sweetness, Sweet, with thee anear.
The names of country, heaven, are changed away
For where thou art or shalt be, there or here;
And this . . . this lute and song . . . loved yesterday,
(The singing angels know) are only dear
Because thy name moves right in what they say.

Elizabeth Barrett Browning (1806–61),
Sonnets from the Portuguese VII

Death of a son
Who died in a mental hospital aged one

Something has ceased to come along with me.
　Something like a person: something very like one.
　　And there was no nobility in it
　　　Or anything like that.

　　Something was there like a one year
　Old house, dumb as stone. While the near buildings
　　Sang like birds and laughed
　　　Understanding the pact

　　They were to have with silence. But he
　Neither sang nor laughed. He did not bless silence
　　Like bread, with words.
　　　He did not forsake silence.

　　But rather, like a house in mourning
　Kept the eye turned in to watch the silence while
　　The other houses like birds
　　　Sang around him.

　　And the breathing silence neither
　　　Moved nor was still.

　　I have seen stones: I have seen brick
　But this house was made up of neither bricks nor stone
　　But a house of flesh and blood
　　　With flesh of stone

And bricks for blood. A house
Of stones and blood in breathing silence with the other
Birds singing crazy on its chimneys.
But this was silence,

There was something else, this was
Hearing and speaking though he was a house drawn
Into silence, this was
Something religious in his silence,

Something shining in his quiet,
This was different, this was altogether something else:
Though he never spoke, this
Was something to do with death.

And then slowly the eye stopped looking
Inward. The silence rose and became still.
The look turned to the outer place and stopped,
With the birds still shrilling around him.
And as if he could speak

He turned over on his side with his one year
Red as a wound
He turned over as if he could be sorry for this
And out of his eyes two great tears rolled, like stones,
and he died.

Jon Silkin (1930–97)

Take him, earth, for cherishing

Take him, earth, for cherishing,
　To thy tender breast receive him.
Body of a man I bring thee,
Noble even in its ruin.

Once was this a spirit's dwelling,
By the breath of God created.
High the heart that here was beating,
Christ the prince of all its living.

Guard him well, the dead I give thee,
Not unmindful of his creature
Shall he ask it: He who made it
Symbol of his mystery.

Come the hour God hath appointed
To fulfil the hope of men,
Then must thou, in very fashion,
What I give, return again.

Not though ancient time decaying
Wear away these bones to sand,
Ashes that a man might measure
In the hollow of his hand:

Not through wandering winds and idle,
Drifting through the empty sky,
Scatter dust was nerve and sinew,
Is it given man to die.

Once again the shining road
Leads to ample paradise;
Open are the woods again
That the serpent lost for men.

Take, O take him, mighty Leader,
Take again thy servant's soul,
To the house from which he wandered
Exiled, erring, long ago.

But for us, heap earth about him,
Earth with leaves and violets strewn,
Grave his name, and pour the fragment
Balm upon the icy stone.

By the breath of God created
Christ the prince of all its living
Take, O take him,
Take him, earth, for cherishing.

Prudentius (348–c.410)

Fear no more the heat o' the sun

Fear no more the heat o' the sun,
    Nor the furious winter's rages;
Thou thy worldly task hast done,
    Home art gone, and ta'en thy wages.
Golden lads and girls all must,
As chimney-sweepers, come to dust.

Fear no more the frown o' the great;
    Thou art past the tyrant's stroke;
Care no more to clothe and eat;
    To thee the reed is as the oak.
The sceptre, learning, physic, must
All follow this, and come to dust.

Fear no more the lightning flash,
    No th' all-dreaded thunder stone;
Fear not slander, censure rash;
    Thou hast finished joy and moan.
All lovers young, all lovers must
Consign to thee, and come to dust.

No exorciser harm thee!
Nor no witchcraft charm thee!
Ghost unlaid forbear thee!
Nothing ill come near thee!
Quiet consummation have;
And renownèd be thy grave!

William Shakespeare (1564–1616), *Cymbeline*

Come softly to my wake

Come softly to my wake
 on Pavlova feet
at the greying end of day;
into the smoke and heat
enter quietly smiling, quietly unknown
among the garrulous guests
gathered in porter nests
to reminisce and moan:
come not with ornate grief
to desecrate my sleep
but a calm togetherness of hands
quiet as windless sands
and if you must weep
be it for the old quick lust
now lost in dust
only you could shake
from its lair.

Come softly to my wake
and drink and break
the rugged crust
of friendly bread
and weep not for me dead
but lying stupidly there
upon the womanless bed
with a sexless stare
and no thought in my head.

Christy Brown (1932–)

No funeral gloom

No funeral gloom, my dears, when I am gone,
  Corpse-gazing, tears, black raiment,
 graveyard grimness;
Think of me as withdrawn into the dimness,
Yours still, you mine; remember all the best
Of our past moments, and forget the rest;
And so, to where I wait, come gently on.
I shall look in the heart of it.

William Allingham (1824–89)

Life goes on

If I should go before the rest of you
  Break not a flower nor inscribe a stone,
Nor when I'm gone speak in a Sunday voice
But be the usual selves that I have known.
    Weep if you must,
    Parting is hell,
    But life goes on,
    So sing as well.

Joyce Grenfell (1910–79)

How did he live?

Not, how did he die, but how did he live?
  Not, what did he gain, but what did he give?
These are the units to measure the worth
Of a man as a man, regardless of birth.
Not what was his church, nor what was his creed?
But had he befriended those really in need?
Was he ever ready, with word of good cheer,
To bring back a smile, to banish a tear?
Not what did the sketch in the newspaper say,
But how many were sorry when he passed away?

Anonymous

O how the mighty have fallen,
in the midst of battle!

Anthem for doomed youth

What passing-bells for these who die as cattle?
  – Only the monstrous anger of the guns.
  Only the stuttering rifles' rapid rattle
  Can patter out their hasty orisons.
No mockeries now for them; no prayers nor bells;
  Nor any voice of mourning save the choirs, –
  The shrill demented choirs of wailing shells;
  And bugles calling them from sad shires.

  What candles may be held to speed them all?
  Not in the hands of boys, but in their eyes
  Shall shine the holy glimmers of goodbyes.
  The pallor of girls' brows shall be their pall;
  Their flowers the tenderness of patient minds,
  And each slow dusk a drawing-down of blinds.

Wilfred Owen (1893–1918)

Let us now sing the praises of famous men

Let us now sing the praises of famous men,
  our ancestors in their generations.
The Lord apportioned to them great glory,
his majesty from the beginning.
There were those who ruled in their kingdoms,
and made a name for themselves by their valour;
those who gave counsel because they were intelligent;
those who spoke in prophetic oracles;

those who led the people by their counsels
and by their knowledge of the people's lore;
they were wise in their words of instruction;
those who composed musical tunes,
or put verses in writing;
rich men endowed with resources,
living peaceably in their homes –
all these were honoured in their generations,
and were the pride of their times.
Some of them have left behind a name,
so that others declare their praise.
But of others there is no memory;
they have perished as though they had never existed;
they have become as though they had never been born,
they and their children after them.
But there were also godly men,
whose righteous deeds have not been forgotten;
their wealth will remain with their descendants,
and their inheritance with their children's children.
Their descendants stand by the covenants;
their children also, for their sake.
Their offspring will continue forever,
and their glory will never be blotted out.
Their bodies are buried in peace,
but their name lives on generation after generation.
The assembly declares their wisdom,
and the congregation proclaims their praise.

Ecclesiasticus (Sirach) 44, the Bible

In Flanders fields

In Flanders fields the poppies blow
  Between the crosses, row on row,
    That mark our place; and in the sky
    The larks, still bravely singing, fly
Scarce heard amid the guns below.

We are the Dead. Short days ago
We lived, felt dawn, saw sunset glow,
    Loved and were loved, and now we lie.
    In Flanders fields.

Take up our quarrel with the foe:
To you from failing hands we throw
    The torch; be yours to hold it high,
    If ye break faith with us who die
We shall not sleep, though poppies grow
    In Flanders fields.

John McCrae (1872–1918)

The soldier

If I should die, think only this of me:
    That there's some corner of a foreign field
That is for ever England. There shall be
    In that rich earth a richer dust concealed;
A dust whom England bore, shaped, made aware,
    Gave, once, her flowers to love, her ways to roam,
A body of England's, breathing English air,
    Washed by the rivers, blessed by suns of home.

And think, this heart, all evil shed away,
    A pulse in the eternal mind, no less
        Gives somewhere back the thoughts by England
            given;
Her sights and sounds; dreams happy as her day;
    And laughter, learnt of friends; and gentleness,
        In hearts at peace, under an English heaven.

Rupert Brooke (1887–1915)

For the fallen

With proud thanksgiving, a mother for her
children,
England mourns for her dead across the sea.
Flesh of her flesh they were, spirit of her spirit,
Fallen in the cause of the free.

Solemn the drums thrill: Death august and royal
Sings sorrow up into immortal spheres.
There is music in the midst of desolation
And a glory that shines upon our tears.

They went with songs to the battle, they were young,
Straight of limb, true of eye, steady and aglow.
They were staunch to the end against odds uncounted,
They fell with their faces to the foe.

They shall grow not old, as we that are left grow old:
Age shall not weary them, nor the years condemn.
At the going down of the sun and in the morning
We will remember them.

They mingle not with their laughing comrades again;
They sit no more at familiar tables of home;
They have no lot in our labour of the day-time;
They sleep beyond England's foam.

But where our desires are and our hopes profound,
Felt as a well-spring that is hidden from sight,
To the innermost heart of their own land they are known
As the stars are known to the Night;

As the stars that shall be bright when we are dust,
Moving in marches upon the heavenly plain,
As the stars that are starry in the time of our darkness,
To the end, to the end, they remain.

Laurence Binyon (1869–1943)

De profundis

Christ, enthroned in highest heaven,
   Hear us, crying from the deep
For the faithful ones departed,
   For the souls of all that sleep;
As thy kneeling Church entreateth,
   Hearken, Shepherd of the sheep.

King of glory, hear our voices,
   Grant the faithful rest, we pray;
We have sinned and may not bide it,
   If thou mark our steps astray,
Yet we plead that saving victim,
   Which for them we bring today.

They are thine, O take them to them;
   Thou their hope, O raise them high;
In thy mercy ever trusting,
   Confident we make our cry
That the souls whom thou hast purchased
   May into thy heart be nigh.

Let thy plenteous loving-kindness
On them evermore be poured;
Let them through thy boundless mercy
Be to boundless life restored,
And within thy Father's mansions
Give to each a place, O Lord.

Where the saints, thy throne surrounding,
Join in the angelic song,
Where thy Mother, raised in glory,
Leads the great redeemed throng,
Grant that we, with souls departed,
May through grace at length belong.

Latin Sequence (13th century)

The arithmetic of death

'May they rest in peace, and may light perpetual shine upon them' – those millions among whom our friends are lost, those millions for whom we cannot choose but pray; because prayer is a sharing in the love of the heart of God, and the love of God is earnestly set towards the salvation of his spiritual creatures, by, through and out of the fire that purifies them.

The arithmetic of death perplexes our brains. What can we do but throw ourselves upon the infinity of God? It is only to a finite mind that number is an obstacle, or multiplicity a distraction. Our mind is like a box of limited content, out of which one thing must be emptied before another can find a place. The universe of creatures is queuing for a turn of our attention, and no appreciable part of the queue will ever get a turn. But no queue forms before the throne of everlasting mercy, because the nature of an infinite mind is to be simply aware of everything that is.

The thought God gives to any of his creatures is not measured by the attention he can spare, but by the object for consideration they can supply. God is not divided; it is God, not a part of God, who applies himself to the falling sparrow, and to the crucified Lord. But there is more in the beloved Son than in the sparrow, to be observed and loved and saved by God. So every soul that has passed out of this visible world, as well as every soul remaining within it, is caught and held in the unwavering beam of divine care. And we may comfort ourselves for our own inability to tell the grains of sand, or to reckon the thousands of millions of the departed.

Austin Farrer (1904–68), *Said or Sung*

Peace

My soul, there is a Country
   Far beyond the stars,
Where stands a winged Sentry
   All skilfull in the wars,
There above noise, and danger
   Sweet peace sits crown'd with smiles,
And one born in a Manger
   Commands the Beauteous files,
He is thy gracious friend,
   And (O my Soul awake!)
Did in pure love descend
   To die here for thy sake,
If thou canst get but thither,
   There grows the flower of peace,
The Rose that cannot wither,
   Thy fortress, and thy ease;
Leave then thy foolish ranges;
   For none can thee secure,
But one, who never changes,
   Thy God, thy life, thy Cure.

Henry Vaughan (1621–95)

Grieve, but not as those
who have no hope

Spring and fall

Márgarét, áre you grieving
  Over Goldengrove unleaving?
Léaves, like the things of man, you
With your fresh thoughts care for, can you?
Áh! ás the heart grows older
It will come to such sights colder
By and by, nor spare a sigh
Though worlds of wanwood leafmeal lie,
And yet you *will* weep and know why.
Now no matter, child, the name.
Sórrow's spríngs áre the same.
Nor mouth had, no nor mind, expressed
What heart heard of, ghost guessed:
It is the blight man was born for,
It is Margaret you mourn for.

Gerard Manley Hopkins (1844–89)

I thought once how Theocritus had sung

I thought once how Theocritus had sung
  Of the sweet years, the dear and wished-for years,
Who each one in a gracious hand appears
To bear a gift for mortals, old or young:
And, as I mused it in his antique tongue,
I saw, in gradual vision through my tears,
The sweet, sad years, the melancholy years,
Those of my own life, who by turns had flung

[59]

A shadow across me. Straightway I was 'ware,
So weeping, how a mystic Shape did move
Behind me, and drew me backward by the hair;
And a voice said in mastery, while I strove, –
'Guess now who holds thee?' – 'Death,' I said. But, there,
The silver answer rang, – 'Not Death, but Love.'

Elizabeth Barrett Browning (1806–61),
Sonnets from the Portuguese I

A grief observed

No one ever told me that grief felt so like fear. I am not afraid, but the sensation is like being afraid. The same fluttering in the stomach, the same restlessness, the yawning. I keep on swallowing.

At other times it feels like being mildly drunk, or concussed. There is a sort of invisible blanket between the world and me. I find it hard to take in what anyone says. Or perhaps, hard to want to take it in. It is so uninteresting. Yet I want the others to be about me. I dread the moments when the house is empty. If only they would talk to one another and not to me.

There are moments, most unexpectedly, when something inside me tries to assure me that I don't really mind so much, not so very much, after all. Love is not the whole of a man's life. I was happy before ever I met H. I've plenty of what are called 'resources'. People get over these things. Come, I shan't do so badly. One is ashamed to listen to this voice but it seems for a little to be making out a good case. Then comes a sudden jab of red-hot memory and all this 'commonsense' vanishes like an ant in the mouth of a furnace.

On the rebound one passes into tears and pathos. Maudlin tears. I almost prefer the moments of agony. These are at least clean and honest. But the bath of self-pity, the wallow, the loathsome sticky-sweet pleasure of indulging it – that disgusts me. And even while I'm doing it I know it leads me to misrepresent H herself. Give that mood its head and in a few minutes I shall have substituted for the real woman a mere doll to be blubbered over. Thank God the memory of her is still too strong (will it always be too strong?) to let me get away with it.

C. S. Lewis (1898–1963), *A Grief Observed*

Think upon death

Think upon death, 'tis good to think of death,
   But better far to think upon the dead.
Death is a spectre with a bony head,
Or the mere mortal body without breath,
The state foredoom'd of every son of Seth,
Decomposition – dust, or dreamless sleep.
But the dear dead are they for whom we weep,
For whom I credit all the Bible saith.

Dead is my father, dead is my good mother,
And what on earth have I to do but die?
But if by grace I reach the blessed sky,
I fain would see the same, and not another;
The very father that I used to see,
The mother that has nursed me on her knee.

Hartley Coleridge (1796–1849)

No worst, there is none

No worst, there is none. Pitched past pitch of grief,
    More pangs will, schooled at forepangs,
        wilder wring.
Comforter, where, where is your comforting?
Mary, mother of us, where is your relief?
My cries heave, herds-long, huddle in the main, a chief
Woe, world-sorrow; on an age-old anvil wince
    and sing –
Then lull, then leave off. Fury had shrieked
    'No lingering!
Let me be fell: force I must be brief'.
O the mind, mind has mountains; cliffs of fall
Frightful, sheer, no-man-fathomed. Hold them cheap
May who ne'er hung there. Nor does long our small
Durance deal with that steep or deep. Here! creep,
Wretch, under a comfort serves in a whirlwind: all
Life death does end and each day dies with sleep.

Gerard Manley Hopkins (1844–89)

On the death of a friend

Grief darkened my heart. Everywhere about me was death. The town became a torment to me, and my own home a prison of unhappiness. All the things that I shared with my dear friend were transformed into cruel torments. My eyes used to look for him everywhere, and he was not there. I grew to hate places we used to frequent simply because he was no longer there. People could no longer say, 'He's on his way' as they used to me when he was alive. I have become a vast enigma to myself. I used to ask my soul why I was so sad, and why his death caused me so much distress. But my soul did not know what reply to give.

I used to weep endlessly and took my rest in bitterness. I was so wretched that I felt a greater attachment to my life of misery than to my dead friend. Although I wanted it to be otherwise, I was more unwilling to lose my misery than him. I found myself weighed down by a sense of being tired of living and scared of dying. I suppose that the more I loved him, the more hatred and fear I felt for death which had taken him from me, as if it were now my keenest enemy. I thought that since death had taken him, it was suddenly going to engulf all humanity.

I was surprised that other people were still alive, since he whom I loved as if he would never die was dead. I was surprised by the fact that he was dead, but I was still alive, because he was my other self. People often say of a friend that he has become 'the other half of their soul'. Well, I felt that my soul and his were one soul living in two bodies. I developed a horror of going on living, because I did not wish to be only half-alive. And perhaps too, that was why I was afraid to die, lest he, whom I loved so much, should die completely.

St Augustine (354–430), *Confessions*

Do not grieve as those who have no hope

We do not want you to be uninformed, brothers and sisters, about those who have died, so that you may not grieve as others do who have no hope. For since we believe that Jesus died and rose again, even so, through Jesus, God will bring with him those who have died. For this we declare to you by the word of the Lord, that we who are alive, who are left until the coming of the Lord, will by no means precede those who have died. For the Lord himself, with a cry of command, with the archangel's call and with the sound of God's trumpet, will descend from heaven, and the dead in Christ will rise first. Then we who are alive, who are left, will be caught up in the clouds together with them to meet the Lord in the air; and so we will be with the Lord for ever. Therefore encourage one another with these words.

First Letter of St Paul to the Thessalonians 4, the Bible

Non piangere, liù

A card comes to tell you
you should report
to have your eyes tested.

But your eyes melted in the fire
and the only tears, which soon dried,
fell in the chapel.

Other things still come –
invoices, subscription renewals,
shiny plastic cards promising credit –
not much for a life spent
in the service of reality.

You need answer none of them.
Nor my asking you for one drop
of succour in my own hell.

Do not cry, I tell myself,
the whole thing is a comedy
and comedies end happily.

The fire will come out of the sun
And I shall look in the heart of it.

Peter Porter (1929–)

Everything passes

Everything passes and vanishes;
    Everything leaves its trace;
And often you see in a footstep
    What you could not see in a face.

William Allingham (1824–89)

Attempts at the rational approach

It isn't in important situations
    that I miss you.
There is always someone who will help
when the toilet floods
or the tiles blow down.
I've learnt to wire a plug,
put up a shelf, to improvise,
make do, or go without.

I have grown a hardened shell
to wear when walking on my own
into restaurants, theatres,
cinemas and bars.

I have grown accustomed
to causing an odd number,
being partnerless at parties,
disturbing symmetry.

Till suddenly I hear the name
of a place we used to visit –
see a snippet in the paper
about an old-time friend –
think up a silly pun
which you would understand . . .

I have learnt new thoughts,
new skills, tested new ventures,
found diversion in a dozen
first-time ways . . .

But when the car-keys disappear
from where I left them,
when next-door's prowling cat
finds an open window,
when the sugarbowl slides off
the kitchen table –
there is no one here to shout at
but myself.

Edna Eglinton

The widower

For a season there must be pain –
   For a little, little space
I shall lose the sight of her face,
Take back the old life again
While She is at rest in her place.

For a season this pain must endure,
For a little, little while
I shall sigh more often than smile
Till Time shall work me a cure,
And the pitiful days beguile.

For that season we must be apart,
For a little length of years,
Till my life's last hour nears,
And, above the beat of my heart,
I hear Her voice in my ears.

But I shall not understand –
Being set on some later love,
Shall not know her for whom I strove,
Till she reach me forth her hand,
Saying, 'Who but I have the right?'
And out off a troubled night
Shall draw me safe to the land.

Rudyard Kipling (1865–1936)

A prayer for his departed wife

O Lord, governor of heaven and earth, in whose hands are embodied and departed spirits, if thou hast ordained the souls of the dead to minister to the living, and appointed my departed wife to have care of me, grant that I may enjoy the good effects of her attention and ministration, whether exercised by appearance, impulses, dreams, or in any other manner agreeable to thy government; forgive my presumption, enlighten my ignorance, and however meaner agents are employed, grant me the blessed influences of thy Holy Spirit; through Jesus Christ our Lord.

Samuel Johnson (1709–84)

Death is nothing at all

Death is nothing at all.
I have only slipped away into the next room.
I am I and you are you.
Whatever we were to each other
    that we still are.

Call me by my old familiar name
Speak to me in the easy way
    which you always used.
Put no difference in your tone.
Wear no forced air of solemnity or sorrow.

Laugh as we always laughed
   at the little jokes we enjoyed together.
Play, smile, think of me; pray for me.
Let my name be ever the household word
   that it always was.
Let it be spoken without affect,
   without the trace of a shadow on it.

Life means all that it ever meant.
It is the same that it ever was.
There is absolutely unbroken continuity.
Why should I be out of mind
   because I am out of sight?

I am waiting for you,
   for an interval,
      somewhere very near,
         just around the corner.

All is well.

Henry Scott Holland (1847–1918)

She is dead

It is hard to have patience with people who say, 'There is no death' or 'Death doesn't matter'. There is death. And whatever is matters. And whatever happens has consequences, and it and they are irrevocable and irreversible. You might as well say that birth doesn't matter. I look up at the night sky. Is anything more certain than that in all those vast times and spaces, if I were allowed to search them, I should nowhere find her face, her voice, her touch? She died. She is dead. Is the word so difficult to learn?

I have no photograph of her that's any good. I cannot even see her face distinctly in my imagination. Yet the odd face of some stranger seen in a crowd this morning may come before me in vivid perfection the moment I close my eyes tonight. No doubt, the explanation is simple enough. We have seen the faces of those we know best so variously, from so many angles, in so many lights, with so many expressions – waking, sleeping, laughing, crying, eating, talking, thinking – that all the impressions crowd into our memory together and cancel out into a mere blur. But her voice is still vivid. The remembered voice – that can turn me at any moment to whimpering child.

C. S. Lewis (1898–1963), *A Grief Observed*

Prayer after stillbirth

God of compassion,
   you make nothing in vain
and love all that you have created:
we commend into your loving hands this child
for whom we longed,
the creation of our love.
You know each of us by name:
call now our child into your loving embrace
where there is life for evermore.
Be gentle with us in our grief.
Protect us from despair,
and give us courage to face tomorrow with hope.

Anonymous

The walk

You did not walk with me
   Of late to the hill-top tree
   By the gated ways,
   As in earlier days;
   You were weak and lame,
   So you never came,
And I went alone, and I did not mind,
Not thinking of you as left behind.

I walked up there today
Just in the former way:
　　Surveyed around
　　The familiar ground
　　By myself again:
　　What difference, then?
Only that underlying sense
Of the look of a room on returning thence.

Thomas Hardy (1840–1928)

Remember

R emember me when I am gone away,
　　Gone far away into the silent land;
　　When you can no more hold me by the hand,
Nor I half turn to go yet turning stay.
Remember me when no more day by day
　　You tell me of our future that you planned:
　　Only remember me; you understand
It will be late to counsel then or pray.
Yet if you should forget me for a while
　　And afterwards remember, do not grieve:
　　For if the darkness and corruption leave
A vestige of the thoughts that once I had,
Better by far you should forget and smile
　　Than that you should remember and be sad.

Christina Rossetti (1830–94)

Do not stand at my grave and weep

Do not stand at my grave and weep;
   I am not there. I do not sleep.
I am a thousand winds that blow.
I am the diamond glints on snow.
I am the sunlight on ripened grain.
I am the gentle autumn rain.
When you awaken in the morning's hush
I am the swift uplifting rush
Of quiet birds in circled flight.
I am the soft stars that shine at night.
Do not stand at my grave and cry;
I am not there. I did not die.

Anonymous

Peace is my parting gift to you

Jesus said to his disciples, 'Do not let your hearts be troubled. Believe in God, believe also in me. In my Father's house there are many mansions. If it were not so, I would have told you. And if I go and prepare a place for you, I will come again and take you to myself, so that where I am, there you may be also. Peace I leave with you, my peace I give to you. Not as the world gives, give I unto you. So let not your hearts be troubled; neither let them be afraid.'

St John's Gospel 14, the Bible

Surprised by joy

Surprised by joy – impatient as the wind
     I turned to share the transport – Oh! with whom
   But thee, deep buried in the silent tomb,
That spot which no vicissitude can find?
Love, faithful love, recalled thee to my mind –
   But how could I forget thee? Through what power,
   Even for the least division of an hour,
Have I been so beguiled as to be blind
To my most grievous loss! – That thought's return
   Was the worst pang that sorrow ever bore,
Save one, one only, when I stood forlorn,
   Knowing my heart's best treasure was no more;
That neither present time, nor years unborn
   Could to my sight that heavenly face restore.

William Wordsworth (1770–1850)

Kontakion for the dead

Give rest, O Christ, to thy servants with thy saints,
     where sorrow and pain are no more,
neither sighing, but life everlasting.

Thou only art immortal, the creator and maker of all:
and we are mortal, formed from the dust of the earth,
and unto earth shalt we return.
For so thou didst ordain when thou createdst me,
   saying,

'Dust thou art, and unto dust shalt thou return.'
All we go down to the dust;
and weeping o'er the grave we make our song:
Alleluia, alleluia, alleluia.

Give rest, O Christ, to thy servants with thy saints,
where sorrow and pain are no more,
neither sighing, but life everlasting.

Russian traditional

Suicide

Why?
 She could have rung me.
Perhaps I should have rung her?
But would it have made any difference?
That night I was out, but she could have left a message,
and I would have phoned back.

I knew she was depressed, but I didn't know it was that
   bad.
Why didn't she say?
She was such a private person.
At times, you know, she just clammed up.
She could be infuriating like that.
I wonder if she died in pain?
I hope not.
God, I'm so angry.

I mean, all she had to do was pick up the phone.
I would have come.

I can't stop thinking about her and wondering.
I keep going over and over it all.
When I shut my eyes I see her face.
Her smile.
Was there a note? I wonder what it said?

I hope she knew I cared.
I really loved her, you know.
Looking back, I wish I had told her that now.
I'm sure she knew, but I just wish I had told her, that's
    all.
Sometimes it wasn't easy to talk.
She had that far away look,
as if imprisoned behind a glass screen.
Remote.

Anonymous

When you were here

When you were here, ah foolish then!
I scarcely knew I loved you, dear.
I know it now, I know it when
You are no longer here.

When you were here, I sometimes tired,
Ah me! that you so loved me, dear.
Now, in these weary days desired,
You are no longer here.

When you were here, did either know
That each so loved the other, dear?
But that was long and long ago:
You are no longer here.

Arthur Symons (1856–1945), *Silhouettes*

Open our graves

God of terror and joy,
you arise to shake the earth.
Open our graves
and give us back the past;
so that all that has been buried
may be freed and forgiven,
and our lives may return to you
through the risen Christ.

Anonymous

You can shed tears that she is gone

You can shed tears that she is gone,
    or you can smile because she has lived.
You can close your eyes and pray that she'll come back,
    or you can open your eyes and see all that she's left.
Your heart can be empty because you can't see her,
    or you can be full of the love you shared.
You can turn your back on tomorrow and live
    yesterday,
or you can be happy for tomorrow because of
    yesterday.
You can remember her and only that she's gone,
    or you can cherish her memory and let it live on.
You can cry and close your mind, be empty and turn
    your back,
or you can do what she'd want: smile, open your eyes,
    love and go on.

Anonymous

Time does not bring relief

Time does not bring relief; you all have lied
    Who told me time would ease me of my pain!
I miss him in the weeping of the rain;
I want him at the shrinking of the tide;
The old snows melt from every mountain-side,
And last year's leaves are smoke in every lane;
But last year's bitter loving must remain
Heaped on my heart, and my old thoughts abide.
There are a hundred places where I fear
To go – so with his memory they brim.
And entering with relief some quiet place
Where never fell his foot or shone his face
I say, 'There is no memory of him here!';
And so stand stricken, so remembering him.

Edna St Vincent Millay (1892–1950)

And death shall have
no dominion

A living hope

Blessed be the God and Father of our Lord Jesus Christ! In his great mercy he has given us a new birth into a living hope through the resurrection of Jesus Christ from the dead, and into an inheritance that is imperishable, undefiled, and unfading, kept in heaven for you. You are being protected by the power of God because you have put your faith in him, until the salvation now in readiness is revealed at the end of time. This is cause for great joy, even if now for a little while you have had to suffer various trials. Even gold passes through the assayer's fire, and much more precious than perishable gold is faith that has stood the test. These trials come so that the genuineness of your faith may be tested, and result in praise and glory and honour when Jesus Christ is revealed. Although you have not seen him, you love him; and even though you do not see him now, you believe in him and rejoice with an indescribable and glorious joy, for you are receiving the outcome of your faith, the salvation of your souls.

First Letter of St Peter 1, the Bible

A sparrow's flight

O ne of King Edwin's chief men offered this advice to the king:

'Your Majesty, it seems to me that a comparison may be drawn between the present life of man here on earth, the duration of which we have no knowledge, and the swift flight of a single sparrow through the banqueting hall where you sit on a winter's night with your thanes and counsellors. In the midst of the hall is a comforting fire which gives warmth to us all; but outside, the storms of winter, rain and snow are raging. A sparrow flies swiftly in through one door of the hall, and out through another. Whilst the bird is inside the hall, it is safe from the winter storms; but after a few moments of comfort, it vanishes from sight, disappearing into the dark wintry world from which it came. And so it is with us. We appear for a little while on the earth. But of what went before this life, and what follows, we know nothing. If this new Christian teaching offers us any more certain knowledge, it seems only sensible that we should follow it.'

And the other elders and counsellors of the king gave him similar advice.

The Venerable Bede (c.670–735),
A History of the English Church and People

Passing away

Passing away, saith the World, passing away:
Chances, beauty and youth sapped day by day:
Thy life never continueth in one stay.
Is the eye waxen dim, is the dark hair changing grey
That has won neither laurel nor bay?
I shall clothe myself in spring and bud in May:
Thou, rootstricken, shall not rebuild thy decay
On my bosom for aye.
Then I answered: Yea.

Passing away, saith my soul, passing away:
With its burden of fear and hope, and labour and play,
Hearken what the past doth witness and say:
Rust in thy gold, a moth in thine array,
A canker is in thy bud, thy leaf must decay.
At midnight, at cockrow, at morning one certain day
Lo, the bridegroom shall come and shall not delay;
Watch thou and pray.
Then I answered: Yea

Passing away, saith my God, passing away:
Winter passeth after the long delay:
New grapes on the vine, new figs on the tender spray,
Turtle calleth to turtle in Heaven's May.
Though I tarry, wait for Me, trust Me, watch and pray:
Arise, come away, night is past, and lo it is day
My love, My sister, My spouse, thou shalt hear me say.
Then I answered: Yea.

Christina Rossetti (1830–94)

The end of delusion

What have I ever seen in this world that hath been truly the same thing that it seemed to me? I have seen marble buildings, and a chip, a crust, a plaster, a face of marble hath pulled off, and I see brick-bowels within. I have seen beauty, and a strong breath from another tells me that that complexion is from without, not from a sound constitution within. I have seen the state of Princes, and all that is but ceremony. As he that fears God, fears nothing else, so he that sees God sees everything else: when we shall see God, we shall see all things as they are. We shall be no more deluded with outward appearances: for, when this sight, which we intend here comes, there will be no delusory thing to be seen. All that we have made as though we saw in this world will be vanished and I shall see nothing but God, and what is in him; and him I shall see in the flesh.

John Donne (1571–1631)

Death is . . .

Death is not the extinguishing of the light but the blowing out of the candle because the dawn has come.

Rabindranath Tagore (1861–1941)

I am your resurrection

He who suspended the earth is suspended,
  He who fastened the heavens is fastened,
He who fixed the universe is fixed on wood,
God has been murdered . . .

God has clothed himself in humanity,
For me a sufferer he has suffered;
For one condemned he has been judged;
For one buried he has been buried;
But he is risen from the dead
And he cries:
Who will plead against me?
I have delivered the one who was condemned,
I have given back life to him who was dead,
I have raised up one who was buried.
Who will dispute my cause? I have abolished death,
I have crushed hell,
I have raised humanity to the highest heavens,
Yes I, the Christ . . .

I am your forgiveness,
I am the Passover of salvation,
I am your light,
I am your resurrection.

Melito of Sardis (died *c*.190), *An Easter Homily*

I am the resurrection and the life

When Jesus arrived, he found that Lazarus had already been in the tomb four days. Now Bethany was near Jerusalem, some two miles away, and many of the Jews had come to Martha and Mary to console them upon their brother's death.

When Martha heard that Jesus was coming, she went and met him, while Mary stayed at home. Martha said to Jesus, 'Lord, if you had been here, my brother would not have died. But even now I know that God will give you whatever you ask of him.' Jesus said to her, 'Your brother will rise again.'

Martha said to him, 'I know that he will rise again in the resurrection on the last day.' Jesus said to her, 'I am the resurrection and the life. Those who believe in me, even though they die, will live, and everyone who lives and believes in me will never die.'

St John's Gospel 11, the Bible

The final awakening

Death, the last sleep?
No, the final awakening.

Sir Walter Scott (1771–1832)

Crossing the bar

Sunset and evening star,
  And one clear call for me!
And may there be no moaning of the bar,
  When I put out to sea,

But such a tide as moving seems asleep,
  Too full for sound and foam,
When that which drew from out the boundless deep
  Turns again home.

Twilight and evening bell,
  And after that the dark!
And may there be no sadness of farewell,
  When I embark;

For though from out our bourne of Time and Place
  The flood may bear me far,
I hope to see my Pilot face to face
  When I have crost the bar.

Alfred, Lord Tennyson (1809–92)

Come to me

Come to me in the silence of the night;
    Come in the speaking silence of a dream;
Come with soft rounded cheeks and eyes as bright
        As sunlight on a stream;
            Come back in tears,
O memory, hope, love of finished years.

O dream how sweet, too sweet, too bitter sweet,
        Whose wakening should have been in Paradise,
Where souls brimful of love abide and meet;
        Where thirsting longing eyes
            Watch the slow door
The opening, letting in, lets out no more.

Yet come to me in dreams, that I may live
        My very life again though cold in death:
Come back to me in dreams, that I may give
        Pulse, breath for breath:
            Speak low, lean low.
As long ago, my love, how long ago!

Christina Rossetti (1830–94)

The loom of time

Man's life is laid in the loom of time
        To a pattern he does not see,
While the weavers work and the shuttles fly
        Till the dawn of eternity.

[90]

Some shuttles are filled with silver threads
       And some with threads of gold,
While often but the darker hues
       Are all that they may hold.

But the weaver watches with skilful eye
       Each shuttle fly to and fro,
And sees the pattern so deftly wrought
       As the loom moves sure and slow.

God surely planned the pattern:
       Each thread, the dark and fair,
Is chosen by his master skill
       And placed in the web with care.

He only knows its beauty,
       And guides the shuttles which hold
The threads so unattractive,
       As well as the threads of gold.

Not till the loom is silent,
       And the shuttles cease to fly,
Shall God reveal the pattern
       And explain the reason why

The dark threads were as needful
In the weaver's skilful hand
As the threads of gold and silver
For the pattern which he planned.

Anonymous

Only an horizon

We seem to give them back, to thee, O God,
    who gavest them to us.
Yet as thou did'st not lose them when thou gavest
    them to us,
so we do not lose them by their return.
Not as the world giveth, givest thou, O Lover of souls.
What thou givest, thou takest not away,
for what is thine is ours also if we are thine.
And life is eternal and love is immortal,
and death is only an horizon,
and an horizon is nothing save the limit of our sight.
Lift us up, strong Son of God,
that we may see further;
draw us closer to thyself,
that we may know ourselves to be nearer to our
    loved ones
who are with thee.
And while thou dost prepare a place for us,
prepare us also for that happy place,
that where thou art there we may be also for evermore.

William Penn (1644–1718), *Fruits of Solitude*

i thank You God for most this amazing day

i thank You God for most this amazing
day:for the leaping greenly spirits of trees
and a blue true dream of sky;and for everything
which is natural which is infinite which is yes

(i who have died am alive again today,
and this is the sun's birthday;this is the birth
day of life and of love and wings:and of the gay
great happening illimitably earth)

how should tasting touching hearing seeing
breathing any–lifted from the no
of all nothing–human merely being
doubt unimaginable You?

(now the ears of my ears awake and
now the eyes of my eyes are opened)

E. E. Cummings (1894–1962)

See, I make all things new

Then I saw a new heaven and a new earth; for the
first heaven and the first earth had passed away,
and the sea was no more. And I saw the holy city, the
new Jerusalem, coming down out of heaven from God,
prepared as a bride adorned for her husband. And I
heard a loud voice from the throne saying, 'See, the home

of God is among mortals. He will dwell with them as their God; they will be his peoples, and God himself will be with them; he will wipe every tear from their eyes. Death will be no more; mourning and crying and pain will be no more, for the first things have passed away.

And the One who was seated on the throne said, 'See, I am making all things new.' Also he said, 'Write this, for these words and trustworthy and true.' Then he said to me, 'It is done! I am the Alpha and the Omega, the beginning and the end. To the thirsty I will give water as a gift from the spring of the water of life. Those who conquer will inherit these things, and I will be their God and they will be my children.'

Revelation 21, the Bible

And all shall be well

On one occasion the good Lord said 'All shall be well.' On another, 'You will see for yourself that all manner of thing shall be well.' In these two sayings the soul discerns various meanings.

One is that God wants us to know that not only does he care for great and noble things, but equally for little and small, lowly and simple things as well. This is his meaning: 'All shall be well.' We are to know that the least will not be forgotten. Another is this: we see deeds done that are so evil, and injuries inflicted that are so great, that it seems to us quite impossible that any good can come of them. As we consider these, sorrowfully and mournfully, we cannot relax in the blessed contemplation of God as we ought.

So from those same six words 'I shall make all things well', I gain great comfort with regard to all the works that God has still to do. There still remains a deed which the blessed Trinity will do at the last day – at least so I see it – yet when and how it will be done is unknown to all God's creatures under Christ, and will remain so until it takes place. The reason why he wants us to know about this deed is that he would have us more at ease in our minds and more at peace in our love, and not be concerned with those storms and stresses that stop us from truly enjoying him.

This great deed, ordained by the Lord God from before time, and treasured and hid within his blessed heart, is known only to himself. By it he will make everything to turn out well. For just as the blessed Trinity made everything out of nothing, in the same way shall he make all that is wrong to turn out for the best.

Julian of Norwich (1373–1417), *Revelations of Divine Love*

25 February 1944

I wish I could believe in something beyond,
  Beyond the death that has undone you.
I wish I could tell of the strength
With which we longed then,
Already drowned,
To walk together once again
Free under the sun.

Primo Levi (1919–87), translated by Eleonora Chiavetta

On dit

Cold is the wind – the flowers below,
  Fearful of winter's hand, lie curled;
But Spring will come again you know,
  And glorify the world.

Dark is the night – no stars or moon;
  But at its blackest, night is done,
All after hastens to the noon,
  The triumph of the sun.

And life is sad, and love is brief.
  Be patient; there will be, they say,
New life, divine beyond belief,
  Somehow, somewhere, some day.

Edith Nesbit (1858–1924)

One another's mystery

So when from hence we shall be gone,
  And be no more, nor you, nor I,
As one another's mystery,
  Each shall be both, yet both but one.

Lord Herbert of Cherbury (1582–1648), *Ode upon a
question moved: whether love should continue forever?*

The Pilgrim's Progress

Then it came to pass, a while after, that there was a
post in the town that inquired for Mr Honest. So he
came to his house where he was, and delivered to his
hand these lines: 'Thou art commanded to be ready
against this day seven-night, to present thyself before thy
Lord, at his Father's house. And for a token that my
message is true, "All thy daughters of music shall be
brought low."' Then Mr Honest called for his friends,
and said unto them, 'I die, but shall make no will. As for
my honesty, it shall go with me; let him that comes after
be told of this.' When the day that he was to be gone was
come, he addressed himself to go over the river. Now the
river at that time overflowed the banks in some places;
but Mr Honest in his lifetime had spoken to one Good-
conscience to meet him there, the which he also did, and
lent him his hand, and so helped him over. The last
words of Mr Honest were, 'Grace reigns.' So he left the
world.

After this it was noised abroad, that Mr Valiant-for-truth was taken with a summons by the same post as the other; and had this for a token that the summons was true, 'That his pitcher was broken at the fountain.' When he understood it, he called for his friends, and told them of it. Then, said he, 'I am going to my Father's; and though with great difficulty I am got hither, yet now I do not repent me of all the trouble I have been at to arrive where I am. My sword I give to him that shall succeed me in my pilgrimage, and my courage and skill to him that can get it. My marks and scars I carry with me, to be a witness for me, that I have fought his battles who now will be my rewarder.' When the day that he must go hence was come, many accompanied him to the river side, into which as he went he said, 'Death, where is thy sting?' And as he went down deeper, he said, 'Grave, where is thy victory?' So he passed over, and all the trumpets sounded for him on the other side.

John Bunyan (1628–88)

The healing judgement of God

The human body is vulnerable to all kinds of illness. Some are relatively easy to treat, others less so. In the case of resistant disease it is sometimes necessary to undergo surgery, cauterization, or to take unpleasant medicine. The same is true of the judgement of God in the next world and the healing of our soul's infirmities.

If we are superficial people, the prospect of such judgement will be experienced as threat: it will be viewed as a process of punishment. On the other hand, the faith of deeper minds will view the prospect of God's judgement as a process of healing, a therapy applied by God in such a way as to restore the being he has created to its original state of grace.

Clearly, it is impossible for doctors to remove boils and tumours from the surface of the body without inflicting pain on their patients; but their intention is not to cause pain, but to bring healing. It is the same when God is confronted with the blemishes that have formed on our soul. At the judgement they will indeed be cut out and removed, but the action will be performed by the gentle wisdom and power of the One who is the physician of the sick.

St Gregory of Nyssa (c.330–94), *Catechetical Oration*

O! come quickly

Never weather-beaten sail more willing bent to
    shore,
  Never tired pilgrim's limbs affected slumber more,
Than my weary spright now longs to fly out of my
    troubled breast.
  O! come quickly, sweetest Lord, and take my soul
    to rest.

Ever blooming are the joys of Heaven's high Paradise.
  Cold age deafs not there our ears, nor vapour dims
    our eyes;
Glory there the sun outshines, whose beams the blessed
    only see.
  O! come quickly, glorious Lord, and raise my spright
    to thee.

Thomas Campion (1567–1620)

Uphill

D oes the road wind uphill all the way?
      Yes, to the very end.
Will the day's journey take the whole long day?
    From morn to night, my friend.

But is there for the night a resting-place?
    A roof for when the slow, dark hours begin.
May not the darkness hide it from my face?
    You cannot miss that inn.

Shall I meet other wayfarers at night?
    Those who have gone before.
Then must I knock, or call when just in sight?
    They will not keep you standing at that door.

Shall I find comfort, travel-sore and weak?
    Of labour you shall find the sum.
Will there be beds for me and all who seek?
    Yea, beds for all who come.

Christina Rossetti (1830–94)

Keep on walking

How happy will be our shout of 'Alleluia' as we enter heaven! How carefree will we be, how secure from attack, where no enemy lurks and no friend dies. There praise is offered to God, and here in this life also; but here it is offered by anxious people, there by those who have been freed from all anxiety; here by those who must die, there by those who will live for ever. Here praise is offered in hope, there by those who enjoy the reality; here by pilgrims in transit, there by those who have reached their homeland.

So let us sing 'Alleluia', although we are not yet in the enjoyment of our heavenly rest, and so sweeten our toil in this life. Let us sing as travellers sing on a journey in order to keep their spirits up. Lighten your toil by singing and never be idle. Sing and keep on walking. And what do I mean by walking? I mean press on from good to better in this life. Persevere, advance in virtue, in true faith and in good living. Sing up – and keep on walking!

St Augustine (354–430)

Bring us at our last awakening

Bring us, O Lord God, at our last awakening into the house and gate of heaven, to enter into that gate and dwell in that house, where there shall be no darkness nor dazzling, but one equal light; no noise nor silence, but one equal music; no fears nor hopes, but one equal possession; no ends nor beginnings, but one equal eternity; in the habitations of thy glory and dominion, world without end.

John Donne (1571–1631)

An old Gaelic blessing

May the road rise to meet you;

May the wind be always at your back;

May the sun shine warm upon your face;

May the rains fall soft upon your fields;

   and until we meet again,

May God hold you in the palm of his hand.

Anonymous

Acknowledgements

Where no acknowledgement is made in the anthology, no source or author is known. Every effort has been made to trace copyright ownership of items included in this anthology. The Author and Publishers apologise to those who have not been traced at the time of going to press, and whose rights who have inadvertently not been acknowledged. They would be grateful to be informed of any omissions or inaccuracies in this respect. The Author and Publisher are grateful for permission to reproduce material under copyright, and are grateful to the following copyright holders:

The Society of Authors, acting on behalf of the Estate of Laurence Binyon, for his poem 'For the Fallen'.

Carlton Publishing Group, on behalf of the Estate of Ogden Nash, for his poem, 'Old men'.

Editions du Seuil and HarperCollins jointly, for an extract from *Le Milieu Divin,* by Pierre Teilhard de Chardin, 1957; ET © Collins, London, 1960.

Elizabeth Barnett (literary executor of the estate of Edna St Vincent Millay), for Edna St Vincent Millay's poems, 'Dirge without music' and 'Time does not bring relief', from *Collected Poems*, HarperCollins Publishers Inc © 1917, 1928, 1945, 1955, Edna St Vincent Millay and Norman Millay Ellis.

Faber & Faber Ltd, for two excerpts from C. S. Lewis, *A Grief Observed*, 1961.

Garzanti Editore and Cassell jointly, for permission to reproduce the poem '25 February 1944' by Primo Levi from *Ad ora incerta*, translated by Eleonora Chiavetta, *Poems on the Underground*, edited by Gerard Benson, Judith Chernaik and Cicely Herbert, Cassell, 1991.

David Higham Associates, for Dylan Thomas' poem, 'Do not go gentle into that good night', first published in *Collected Poems*, Dent, 1953.

Shiel Land Associates Ltd, on behalf of the Trustees of Joyce Grenfell's Estate, for her poem, 'Life Goes On', *Joyce: By Herself And Her Friends*, Macmillan, 1980; © The Joyce Grenfell Memorial Trust, 1980.

W. W. Norton & Company, for the poem 'i thank You God for most this amazing day', *Collected Poems 1934–1963*, E. E. Cummings, edited by George J. Firmage © 1991 by the Trustees for the E. E. Cummings Trust and George James Firmage.

Peter Porter, for his poem, 'Non piangere liù', *Collected Poems*, Oxford University Press, 1989.

The Random House Group Limited, for Christy Brown's poem, 'Come softly to my wake' *Collected Poems*, Secker & Warburg.

Brian Read, for Arthur Symons' poem, 'When you were here', *Collected Poems*, William Heinemann & Co © Literary Executor of Arthur Symons.

Mrs Jon Silkin, for her late husband's poem, 'Death of a Son', *Poems New and Selected,* first published by Wesleyan University Press, USA, 1966.

St Paul's (formerly St Paul Publications), UK, for an extract from Cardinal Basil Hume, *To be a Pilgrim,* 1984.

Index of Biblical Readings

Unless stated, quotations are taken from the *New Revised Standard Version* © 1989 The Division of Christian Education of the National Council of Churches in the USA.

Index of Authors

Index of Titles or First Lines

[113]

What passing-bells for these who die as cattle? 47
When I am dead, my dearest 32
When to the sessions of sweet silent thought 7
When you were here, ah foolish then 78
With proud thanksgiving, a mother for her children 51

You can shed tears that she is gone 79
You did not walk with me 72